Rebound 1976

THE PEARL

THE PEARL

The Fourteenth Century English Poem

Rendered in Modern Verse

With an Introductory Essay by

STANLEY PERKINS CHASE

New York

Oxford University Press

1932

Printed in the United States of America

To

H. J. C.

I sette hyr sengeley in syngulere.

Foreword

A TRANSLATOR of this poem must of necessity feel a sense of deep obligation to those many scholars whose pioneer labours have made his task at all possible, especially to the editors of the two critical editions, Professor Charles G. Osgood, of Princeton University, and the late Sir Israel Gollancz, of King's College, London. The former has encouraged me by his interest in the progress of my work. The latter had died before my task was undertaken, but I remember with pleasure the many kindnesses which he and Lady Gollancz showed me, several years ago, when I was living in London. In both the translation and the critical study there doubtless remain errors and inadequacies of various kinds, for which I alone am responsible; there would be more of these but for the generous help which I have received, and which I here would gratefully acknowledge, from Mr. Herbert

Hartman, Mr. C. H. Gray, and other friends and colleagues. I wish to record my hearty thanks also to my former teachers, Professor G. L. Kittredge and President William Allan Neilson, who read the translation in manuscript and made a number of valuable suggestions. Most of all I owe to the clear discernment and the delicate taste of my wife, whose book this is.

S. P. C.

Bowdoin College,
October 26, 1932.

Contents

[ix]

Introduction

THE present rendering of this fourteenth century poem is not intended primarily for students of that period (though I permit myself to hope that it may please some of them), but for readers of poetry in general. Therefore it will not be amiss to restate here the most pertinent facts, so far as they are known, concerning the language, the poetic form, and the authorship of the original work, the intellectual and religious influences bearing upon it, and something of its place in literary history. In its main purport, however, and without regard to subtleties of interpretation, the poem is so clear and so self-sufficient that the reader who is making his first acquaintance with it may be counselled to turn directly to the translation.

I

The poem called *The Pearl* (it is without title in the only extant manuscript) has been known to scholars for nearly a hundred years. It has been generally accessible only since 1891, when Professor Gollancz published his first edition, provided with a

critical apparatus and a modern rendering,
and graced with a felicitous quatrain by the
aged Laureate of the Victorian era:

> We lost you — for how long a time —
> True Pearl of our poetic prime!
> We found you, and you gleam re-set
> In Britain's lyric coronet.

Since that date, the poem has been twice
edited — by Professor Charles G. Osgood
in 1906 and by Sir Israel Gollancz again in
1921.[1] It has been rendered in modern English, prose or verse, at least nine times, and it
has even been translated once into Italian. In-
creasingly of late it has been the subject of
commentary and discussion.

The reasons for such continued and wide-
spread interest are not hard to understand,
Any student of the period will acknowledge
the claim which *The Pearl* has upon our attention as perhaps the purest expression in
mediaeval English literature of that utter
spiritual humility and devotion which were,
at least ideally, the fruits of its religious dis-

[1] Chiefly as an experiment in the printing of the text with
modern letters substituted for the obsolete characters of Middle English, but embodying also the results of recent textual
criticism, the Bowdoin Edition of the poem was published
in 1932. (For reference to books and articles mentioned in
this Introduction, see the Bibliography, pp. 107-110.)

cipline. In technique the poem is equally interesting, though far less representative by reason of the intricacy of its verse-form; indeed, it is saved from sheer artificiality only by an unfailing freshness and genuineness of poetic inspiration. It presents, for those who care for such inquiries, the fascination of a still unsolved problem of authorship, involving the relation between this work and the finest of the English romances, *Sir Gawain and the Green Knight*. And concerning *The Pearl* itself there confronts one a question of interpretation which has engaged many acute and learned minds: is it fundamentally an elegy upon the death of a dearly loved child? or an allegory of an abstract type, rendered intimate and personal by the genius of the poet? or a record in figurative language of the private spiritual experience of a religious? From whichever side one comes to it, the poem is deserving of study, and, I think, of still further effort to render it adequately in modern English.

For the language of the original is not without difficulty even to those who can read Chaucer with ease. It has usually been described as West Midland, sometimes as the dialect of the extreme Northwest Midland; but scholars now hesitate to fix geographical limits with precision. One recent student, in support of his attribution of the poem to John de Erghome, has argued that its language is that of Yorkshire rather than of the Northwest. Distinctly Northern peculiarities of speech, especially many words of Scandinavian origin, have been accounted for by infiltration of such forms into the Midland area from neighbouring districts where Danish influence upon the language had been strong. Whatever its locality, the dialect differs considerably from the East Midland of Chaucer, especially in its vocabulary. A good many of the words are unusual, either obsolete to-day or surviving chiefly in dialects; some are to be recognized only by their Scandinavian analogues. The poem employs freely also the Romance words which had come into English within the preceding two centuries, as well as the large stock of native words in forms differing only slightly from those used by Chaucer. A vocabulary of such diverse elements, which well illustrates the fluid and emergent character of English at this period, gives to the language of *The Pearl* a surprising richness and copiousness. At the same time, it precludes any wide popularity to-day for the poem in its original form.

In a unique manuscript of the late fourteenth century, which may be seen by any visitor to the British Museum, are preserved four unsigned poems, *The Pearl*,[2] *Patience*, *Cleanness* (or *Purity*), and *Sir Gawain and the Green Knight.* The fact that these poems, thus bound together, show the same dialectal characteristics and marked similarities in vocabulary has led scholars generally to assume common authorship for the four, despite the differences between them. *Patience* and *Cleanness* are paraphrases of Biblical material: the first, a fairly concise rendering of the story of Jonah, as an exemplar of the virtue of patience; the second, which in its proportions approaches epic, a series of three Old Testament narratives (the Flood, the Destruction of Sodom and Gomorrah, and the Downfall of Belshazzar), selected to illustrate the punishment which God visits on those who defile themselves with any kind of uncleanness. Both poems are written

[2] So entitled by the first editor, Richard Morris.

in long, alliterative, unrhymed lines. In the fourteenth century, this accentual prosody, native to English verse (though the Middle English employment of it differs markedly from the Anglo-Saxon), was being revived for literary purposes by a group of writers who, living in the West and North of England, were less subject to Court fashions in verse than were men like Chaucer and Gower. The two Biblical paraphrases are vigourous, masculine works; *Cleanness* especially, though somewhat ill-proportioned, shows a good deal of narrative power, a feeling for beauty, and at moments a vein of tenderness and lyric sweetness. In both poems we miss the delicacy, grace, distinction of phrase, which are preëminent traits of *Gawain* and *The Pearl*. Their moral earnestness, however, especially the passion for purity which appears in *Cleanness*, is akin to that of the other two poems; and their rather oppressively homiletic character may be explained by the subject-matter which the poet had here chosen and the more directly practical aim which he had in view. Even between the two superior poems, notwithstanding an underlying affinity, there are striking differences. With great nobility, *Gawain* sets forth the ideal of Christian knighthood; yet this exposition is in the form of a courtly romance, and the outlook and atmosphere of the poem are predominantly secular. *The Pearl* impresses us at once as the work of a cleric, or, at all events, of a man deeply in sympathy with the religious life, versed in its literature, experienced in its special difficulties and its great consolations. Like the two didactic works, *Gawain* is written in the long, unrhymed lines of the Northern school, but these are grouped in strophes of irregular length, and each strophe ends with a "bob and wheel" (five short lines, rhymed, in a special arrangement). This introduction into the epic alliterative measure of a lyrical burden characteristic of the rhymed romances of the South effects an interesting combination of the two systems of prosody, native and foreign, then current in England. A more thorough-going and intricate union of the two is seen in the stanzaic form of *The Pearl*, description of which may be postponed to a later paragraph.

Efforts to discover the poet's name have had, as yet, no sure success. Earlier attributions to the Scottish Huchown of the Awle Ryale and to the Londoner Ralph Strode have proved unconvincing. The tentative nomination[3] of the secular clerks John Donne and John Prat rests upon a series of precarious conjectures, including the highly uncertain assumption that *The Pearl* was written in memory of a girl named Margaret. Mr. C. O. Chapman's recent suggestion that the author may have been the Augustinian Friar of York, John de Erghome, has, it seems to me, much more to commend it than any previous attribution; but this interesting proposal, acceptance of which necessitates the relinquishment of earlier conclusions about the language and the locality, must await the fuller examination of scholars and the possible uncovering of fresh evidence.

Meanwhile, we must continue to refer to the author of these notable poems as "the Pearl poet" or "the Gawain poet." He lived in the second half of the fourteenth century: his works cannot be dated more precisely than as composed between 1360 and 1400. About him we know with certainty nothing

[3] By Oscar Cargill and Margaret Schlauch.

[xviii]

except what may be gleaned from the poems themselves. "Readers of the *Gawain*," writes Osgood,[4] "find various phases of life about a feudal castle brought before them in many vivid and minute details. The splendor and delight of feast in hall, the tapestries and furnishings, the knight's chamber, his armament, the devotions of the household, the day spent indoors or without, the hunt in all its episodes varied according to the game— these have all evidently been at some time every-day matters to the poet, and he describes them with lively but innocent enthusiasm." Moreover, he was, we feel, no inferior or mere onlooker, but one who moved naturally and by right in gentle society. Sensitive to the varying aspects of nature in his northern shire, he has given us descriptions of summer fields, of moonrise, of the movement of water, of bleak winter landscapes, and of storm-swept crags, remarkable for their power and beauty. His evident appreciation of secular music bears out the impression that he must have been connected at some time with a great household; and his somewhat technical knowledge of church

[4] Ed. *Pearl*, x. Cf. also Gollancz ed., xli-xlii.

music suggests his probable training as a boy in a choristers' school attached to cathedral, monastery, or parish church.[5]

Clearly, he was familiar with polite French literature—in particular, with the *Roman de la Rose*. Much of the literary machinery of this allegory (the dream; the vision; the trees, birds, flowers, rivulets, of the landscape) he employs in *The Pearl*; and once, in *Cleanness*, he refers to Jeun de Meun at some length. We are uncertain whether he knew the work of that other admirer of the *Roman de la Rose*—his great London contemporary, Geoffrey Chaucer. With the latter's *Book of the Duchess*, composed in 1369, *The Pearl* shares nothing more than certain general characteristics of elegy and dream-vision. *The Pearl* has some points of likeness also to a Latin eclogue, *Olympia*, which Boccaccio wrote in memory of a young daughter. And with a far greater dream-vision poem than either the *Book of the Duchess* or *Olympia* —namely, Dante's *Divine Comedy*—*The Pearl* undoubtedly has, within limits, a certain affinity; but this is a matter of the habitual modes of thought and feeling in the Mid-

[5] Cf. Chapman (I).

dle Ages rather than of direct influence. The English poem has nothing of the intellectual range and power of Dante's masterpiece. It cannot be proved, and on the whole I think it is unlikely, that the Pearl poet knew the work of either Boccaccio or Dante. He was plainly a highly educated person, of cultivated tastes as attested by his fondness for the chivalric romances; but his studies had probably been in the direction of theology, homiletics, and mysticism rather than of secular literature, classical or modern. Above all, his mind, like Langland's in his own century, like Spenser's and Bunyan's in later centuries, was steeped in the language and imagery of the Bible.

Of his religious interests and tendencies we can make out a good deal. Some study of the theological controversies of the age, and a decided attitude toward at least one of them, are implicit in the middle portion of *The Pearl*—though he touches the theme more in the manner of the poet than of the disputant. Except for his stand on this one matter,[6] his tendencies led him to side with the conservative, or Augustinian, school of

[6] Cf. p. xxxvi below, and Carleton Brown.

theologians, represented by Bishop Bradwardine, against the Pelagian. With the contemporary practice of mysticism[7] which flourished in the monasteries and convents of the North of England, and which produced at least one classic of religious literature, *The Imitation of Christ* by Thomas à Kempis, he was in deep accord. There is in him no trace of the morbidity which runs through the work of one prominent member of that group, Richard Rolle of Hampole; nor, on the other hand, has he much of the temper of a reformer—a Langland or a Wycliffe. He seems to have been a man "eager to inspire enthusiasm for permanent ideals rather than to remedy in special cases the results of dishonor or vice."[8] But attempts to construct anything like a biography on the basis of the extant poems are merely fanciful; in this brief introduction, we may profitably forgo them, and turn to a closer examination of our poem. It will be worth while to make a somewhat detailed analysis, confining ourselves to what the poem indubitably

[7] Cf. Sister Madeleva, Ch. III.
[8] Schofield (II), 203.

says and keeping clear, for the present, of all major implications and in-readings.

II

The two opening lines, after the manner of a mediaeval lapidary, are an apostrophe to pearls in the generic or abstract sense, praising them for the quality of purity which makes them so dear to princes. Immediately the poet mentions one particular pearl, precious above all others, which had been the source of all his happiness. But he has lost this treasure; in a garden-plot it slipped from his hands, rolled through the grass, and disappeared in the earth. Since that time he has known no joy, and is given over to sorrow and heaviness. One day in August, in "a high season" (perhaps the Feast of the Assumption), he goes to the spot, now covered with pleasant herbs and flowers, where the pearl had slipped from him; in his grief over his loss, his will in rebellion against God, he sinks to the ground. Soon, overcome by the sweetness of the odours that assail his senses, he falls asleep and begins to dream. The rest of the poem, until near the end, is all within the dream.

THE PEARL

The poet finds himself transported (stanza 6) to a region of supernal beauty and wonder—of gleaming cliffs, trees of blue boles and silver foliage, hung with fragrant fruit, birds of brilliant plumage and sweet note, and a rivulet whose banks shine with all kinds of precious stones, the very gravel of whose shores is of orient pearls. His grief forgotten, eagerly and gladly he follows this stream, but with his eyes fixed upon the region beyond it, to which he would cross but for the depth of the water, for it is of even greater splendour, and he feels instinctively that Paradise is there—the towers of the City but concealed by some slope of ground. Then (stanza 14) he sees, seated on the opposite side of the stream, a maiden, demure and beautiful, dressed all in white, her robe adorned with pearls, a crown of mother-of-pearl on her head, and, gleaming on her breast, the most wonderful pearl he has ever seen. Instantly he recognizes her as one he has known before; and as she rises and approaches him across the stream, this recognition becomes ever the surer and the more joyful, for, says the poet, "she was nearer to me than aunt or niece." With high-bred courtesy and unconcealed delight, the maiden greets him, and the dreamer addresses her.

There follows a long conversation between them, which takes up almost exactly three-fifths of the poem—from stanza 21 to stanza 82. The dreamer's first request is for reassurance: is she indeed the pearl whose loss he has mourned so long? What cruel fate could have stolen his treasure from him, leaving him in a prison of grief, while she has been enjoying the delights of Paradise? Quietly the maiden corrects him both for his causeless grief and for the accusations he has brought against his "wyrd" or fate. What he lost was but an ephemeral, transitory thing, like a rose; the coffer that held his pearl, she somewhat cryptically adds, has made it a pearl of price. He should be grateful to his "wyrd," which has thus "made something out of nothing" for him. In his reply (stanza 24), he assumes that, having recovered his pearl, he is to be separated from it no more; he would cross the stream forthwith and join her, his Pearl, in that sunny grove. But again she rebukes him for his presumption. Authoritatively, and with a kind of mild, cloistral humour, turned like a stream of coolness upon his hot impatience, she points out three errors that he has made in a single brief speech. In assuming that she is really where he sees her to be, he has accepted the fallible testimony of his senses; secondly, he has taken for granted that he is to live with her forever; and thirdly, he has light-heartedly talked of crossing a stream which no man may pass before he dies.

Thus rebuffed, the dreamer (stanza 28) falls again into lamentation and reckless outcry, from which he is recalled by the maiden's reminder that God's judgements are not to be swayed by man's complaints; she urges him to submit to God and throw himself wholly upon His mercy. Humbled by her words, the dreamer asks God's forgiveness, and begs the Pearl to tell him something of the circumstances, "early and late," of her heavenly life. She replies (stanza 34) that, although she was "of tender age" when she arrived there, she was at once taken in marriage by the Lamb and crowned as queen, as he now sees her. The dreamer (stanza 36) is astonished, for he knows that Mary is Queen of Heaven: how should a newcomer supplant the Queen unless she excelled the Virgin herself? His very mention of such a possibility, innocently as it was uttered, brings the maiden to her knees in humble supplication to that "matchless Mother and merriest May." After an interval of devotion, she explains that the Kingdom of Heaven harbours no usurpers; everyone who enters there is a king or a queen, and Mary is the Empress over them all. The "courtesy" of the Kingdom is analogous to that subordination of the members which St. Paul explained; there is in Heaven no rancour or jealousy on the part of the co-equal sovereigns either toward one another or toward their honoured Empress.

Still the dreamer cannot reconcile himself to such apparent denial of elementary laws of justice as would seem to be involved in the Pearl's advancement to the rank of queen. Bluntly he reminds her (stanza 41) that she had lived "not two years in our company," and knew neither Creed nor Paternoster. Her qualifications might entitle her to sit in Heaven as a countess, or a lady of lower rank, but surely, surely not as a queen!

The ensuing speech of the Pearl (stanzas 42-48) is a lively rendering of the parable of the labourers in the vineyard, a favourite passage with mediaeval exegetists in discussions of the question whether rewards in Heaven were equal or proportionate. The application of the parable here, of course, is to the maiden's own case. She is among those who "came into the vineyard at eventide"; as the dreamer had said in his more literal fashion, she had lived less than two years among his folk: yet at the first possible moment (when the labourers were paid at the end of the day, or when she first arrived in the Kingdom) she had received her wages in full. Uncompromisingly she proclaims that spiritual rewards (the "bliss" and "joy" of Heaven) do not conform to the principles of earthly recompense. Each man's prize is there the same, whatever the length or the severity of his trial may have been.

Still the dreamer is unconvinced. Such distribution of heavenly favours, regardless of what seem to him plain inequalities of merit, outrages his sense of justice. Citing text for text (stanza 50), he quotes from the *Psalms*, "Thou renderest to every man according to his work," and suggests that the logical outcome of the system she has described would be a constantly increasing stipend for less and less work ("and ever the longer, the less the more").

Patiently the Pearl answers him, point by point; this part of the poem is, in structure, like a mediaeval debate, or *disputatio*. Would he really be willing to be judged by desert or merit alone? Are the holiest men so free from sin that they are thereby assured of salvation? In a single stanza (54) she outlines for the dreamer the whole plan of redemption, which depends ultimately not upon one's good works, but upon the freely offered grace of God through the sacrifice of Christ. Within certain limitations, she recognizes the importance of good works or "righteousness"; at one point (stanza 58) she glances at the experience of Jacob as a type of the man who atones for sin by repentance and good deeds. In general, her argument runs, there are two ways by which to attain salvation, two kinds of claim that may be presented for God's recognition: the claim of the "righteous" and the claim of the "innocent." Of these, the first, as has been shown, is by far the more frail and uncertain; the second, blamelessness of life, is the

way that all should seek. For while the re-
pentant sinner may, through God's mercy,
be forgiven and received, the innocent has
an irrefragable claim founded upon the nature of God Himself.

> For God the judgement never gave
> That guiltless souls have punishment.

Intellectually this is the central theme of
the poem—the exaltation of purity. It has
been supported by keen dialectic; now it is
to be enforced by the plain words of Our
Lord Himself and by that tenderest of Gospel narratives, His blessing of the little children—"for of such is the Kingdom of Heav-
en." Innocence, sinlessness—such too was the
significance of that other pearl, for which
the "jeweller" of Scripture sold all his goods;
and, as the maiden recalls, Christ Himself
said that that pearl of great price was also a
symbol of the Kingdom. Ending her long
discourse with a gesture which one feels to
be the true crisis or turning-point of the
poem (stanza 62), the maiden points to the
resplendent pearl on her own breast, set
there "in token of peace" by the Lamb, and
counsels the dreamer to forsake "the mad
world" and purchase for himself the pearl
of price.

INTRODUCTION

The dialectical part of the poem is ended;
the theme has been raised above the plane of
argument and dispute; and when the dreamer speaks again, it is in a new and chastened
tone. He would know who made the glorious being he sees, for of Nature's creation
she cannot be, and he would know more spe-
cifically the office or function of the spotless
pearl she has shown him. In a lyrical passage
(stanza 64) echoing the *Song of Songs*, she
replies that, when she left our dark, misty
world, the Lamb of God called her to be
His bride. The dreamer, though no longer
combative, is still naïve; he pictures her as a
matchless maid, strong and brave, triumph-
ing in battle over all her rivals. But the Pearl
again insists that, though she is spotless, she
has not claimed to be "matchless," and she
reminds him of the vision in which St. John
saw the hundred and forty-four thousand
virgins on Mount Sion, all alike arrayed in
wedding garments. To this company she herself belongs. Here (stanza 66) is the first, almost incidental mention of the Apocalyptic
vision to which the whole poem is leading
up. The tone and movement have become
more lyrical, more ecstatic, though the firm

logical plan of the whole is never impaired.
The dreamer has asked the maiden (stanza
65) a question about the nature of the Lamb
—what kind of being He is. Her reply (stanzas 67-70) takes the form of a citation of
the three chief Scriptural passages in which
the Saviour is represented as a Lamb—the
prophecy of Isaiah, the prophecy of St. John
the Baptist, and (again a reference to *Revelation*) the vision in which John of Patmos
saw Him opening the book with the seven
seals. This third passage should convince the
dreamer of the truth of that which he has
been so slow to understand: the communal
nature of heavenly bliss. To make the teach-
ing still more explicit, the Pearl paraphrases
for him the words of the vision itself (stanzas 73-75).

Understanding at last the lesson she has
imparted, rendered timorous by the percep-
tion of her utter purity and the sense of
his own uncleanness, the dreamer (stanza
76) has but one further request—an earnest
prayer that he may see her dwelling-place,
for he knows that she is but sojourning here
by the brook. It cannot be that Jerusalem,
the city of which she has spoken, lies near-

INTRODUCTION

by; where then, and in what manner of dwelling, does she live? His schooling is not quite completed: he must have explained to him the difference between the Old and the New Jerusalem (stanzas 79-80). As for his request to enter the City, that is not God's pleasure. The Pearl, however, has obtained from the Lamb, as a special boon, permission to show the dreamer the outer walls of that sacred enclosure, and she directs him to follow along the side of the brook, opposite to her, until he comes to a hill. Here ends the long dialogue.

From the hill, spread out before him, the dreamer (stanza 82) sees in vision the New Jerusalem. The description of the Holy City is drawn from the account given of it in the Apocalypse, including the twelve precious stones of the foundation, the walls of jasper, four-square and transparent, the gates of pearl, the golden streets, the throne, the river, the trees of life. One significant detail the poet adds to the Biblical account: the "dwellings" within the City, about which the dreamer has inquired, are seen by him, all resplendent with jewels. This concluding part of the vision owes much of its moving

power, of course, to the magnificence and
the emotional associations of the chapters in
Revelation; but the poet has rendered his
original with impressiveness, improving upon
it sometimes by his selection and arrangement of material, and he has given to his narrative a startling dramatic quality. Steadily
the emotional stress is increased as the reader
is carried from one intense moment of the
experience to another. I know few finer reti-
cences in literature than that with which
the poet leaves unattempted any description
of the Presence of God:

> The High God's Self sat on the Throne.

Momentarily thereafter (stanza 91) the
dreamer attains the state of pure ecstasy,
without sense either of exertion or of rest.

One does not see how the dream can well
be carried further. But, introduced by a
comparison to moonrise which is surely
among the remarkable similes of English poetry, there succeeds to this mystical trance a
scene of great animation, when the City is
suddenly filled with the hosts of the Lamb,
moving in procession, and the Heavens re-
sound with their song. There, among the redeemed, the dreamer sees his "little queen,"

whom he had thought still near him by the brook. Desperate with longing, he rushes headlong toward the water, intending to swim across to her—and the violence of that movement awakens him from the dream. He is still lying on the bank in the herb-garden where he had fallen asleep. Bewildered, heart-broken from disappointment, he falls at first into "great affright"; and then, recovering himself, he meditates on the lesson which this "true dream" has brought him: the lesson of the entire submission of the human will to the Divine:

> Now all be to that Prince's pleasure.

The closing stanza is an expression of true Christian humility and devotion; it ends with a prayer that we may all be His "homly hyne" (servants of the household) and precious pearls unto His pleasure.

III

The interpretation of the poem which probably still commands the most general support is that, in its main intention, it is an elegy expressing grief over the loss of a two-year-old child and the consolation afforded by a heavenly vision in which she is seen as a

Bride of the Lamb. Into the elegiac frame-
work, according to this interpretation, the
poet has introduced various other elements,
suggested by or related to the central experience, such as praise of innocence, discussion
of the status in Heaven of baptized infants,
the doctrine of the equality of heavenly rewards, and the exhortation to submission and
humility. That the poem voices a grief so intimate and personal that it could have been
written only by a sorrowing father was the
conviction of both editors, as well as of many
commentators, and has been assumed by all
previous verse-translators except Miss Weston. It has been pointed out[9] that the poet
champions a view of the equality of heavenly rewards and an interpretation of the
parable of the labourers in the vineyard in
conflict with the opinions of the leading theological authorities of his age. In this insistence upon the doctrine of equal rewards
Mr. Osgood sees a father's passionate con-
cern over the heavenly state of his lost in-
fant daughter. The pearl which the poet has
lost, then, represents the little child who

[9] By Carleton Brown, who, however, does not commit
himself to the autobiographic interpretation.

died;[10] the garden-green to which the grief-stricken father repairs is the spot where she lies buried; the maiden who appears to him in vision is the soul of his loved one, now grown to full stature in Heaven; and the message which she gives him conveys both reassurance upon the intellectual difficulty which has tormented his mind and a counsel of submission to the will of God.

Such an interpretation has been fitted to the autobiographic inferences that may be drawn from the other works of the author and from *The Pearl* itself. That he had a child at all—at least, one whom he publicly acknowledged—would indicate that he was not a priest or a monk throughout his mature life. We may assume, then, that he was a layman and married, though there is in the poem no reference, direct or implied, to the mother of the child. Did he, perhaps, enter the religious life late—possibly as the result of a spiritual crisis occasioned by his bereavement? But *Patience* and *Cleanness*, which on grounds of style we should date earlier than

[10] A favourite corollary to this interpretation is that the word Pearl ("margery" in older English) indicates that the child's name was Margaret, Marguerite, or Margery.

The Pearl, show an equal preoccupation with moral and religious matters; and *Gawain*, which is the most mature of the four in literary art, is also the most secular. Thus a chronology of the poet's works is not easy to accommodate to the supposition that he was a layman drawn into the religious vocation by a desolating personal bereavement. It is not strictly necessary, however, to assume, and neither Gollancz nor Osgood does so, that the poet was ever an ecclesiastic.[11] As Gollancz suggests, he may have studied divinity at some university or monastic school; but interest in theological questions was by no means confined, in the fourteenth century, to those preparing for or already in orders, as Chaucer's works abundantly demonstrate.

Not all commentators who accept the elegiac interpretation have been convinced that the loss which is the subject of the poem was the poet's own.[12] We have been reminded that poems (Chaucer's *Book of the Duchess* is an instance) were often written for a pa-

[11] Schofield, Carleton Brown, and Sister Madeleva all believe that he was an ecclesiastic.

[12] E.g., Cargill and Schlauch.

tron, commemorating some experience of
the latter, or voicing some sentiment which
it was thought more delicate to express in an
indirect way. A genuine poet might well
find such an external stimulus sufficient to
arouse his highest powers of feeling and expression. Much other literature should warn
us against the danger of too narrowly autobiographic an interpretation of some record-
ed experience simply because it seems to have
been so poignantly felt. In this second view,
the daughter, the father, the bereavement,
the grief, and the consolation may all have
been actual, or have had their foundation in
an actual experience; but the poetic rendering of the experience is the work of some
one else than the principal figure concerned.
If we assume the relation to have been that
of patron and poet, there is nothing to pre-
clude our fancying that the latter may himself have known and loved the child whose
loss he commemorates.

The two chief remaining interpretations
it is less easy to summarize adequately for
the reason that they depend so largely upon
comparisons with other bodies of literature
and upon modes of thought not habitual to

our age. The first critic definitely to challenge the autobiographic-elegiac view was the late Professor W. H. Schofield. In two extremely learned and fully documented essays, he demonstrated, first, the very wide popularity of the mediaeval "lapidary," or book of gems, with its more or less conventional formulas for the description of precious stones, and in particular he showed the vogue of the pearl. The fourteenth century felt strongly the sentiment which two modern writers have thus expressed:

Unlike other gems, the pearl comes to us perfect and beautiful, direct from the hand of nature. Other precious stones receive careful treatment from the lapidary, and owe much to his art. The pearl, however, owes nothing to man. Perhaps this has much to do with the sentiments we cherish for it. It touches us with the same sense of simplicity and sweetness as the mountain daisy or the wild rose. It is absolutely a gift of nature on which man cannot improve.[13]

Naturally, this wide-spread admiration of the pearl was reflected in literature, and, naturally in that age, the object so admired was allegorized. In fact, says Schofield, the literary use of the pearl for symbolical or allegorical purposes, especially its association

[13] Kunz and Stevenson, *Book of the Pearl* (London, 1908), 305. Quoted by Schofield (II), 643.

with virginity, had become so common that
the mere choice of such a subject for a poem
almost amounted to apprising the reader that
he was to expect an allegorical treatment.
Attacking as mere guess-work the construc-
tions which had previously been put upon
The Pearl, the critic emphasized the facts
that the poet nowhere calls the child his
daughter; that he fails to give us any clear
idea of her earthly appearance or life or sur-
roundings; that he never mentions the mother or any other persons who would have
mourned her untimely death; and that the
tone of the Pearl-maiden toward the dreamer throughout most of their conversation is
lacking in that filial affection for which a
bereaved parent would surely yearn.

To Schofield the Pearl-maiden was "merely an allegorical figure, a being purely and
simply of the poet's imagination,"—no more
an actual person than the divine lady who
reasoned with Boethius in his prison-cell, or
the Rose which Guilliaume de Lorris sought
to pluck. The poet's general idea, he held,
was to celebrate the virtue of chastity;
"above all, to exalt the purity of the maiden,
. . . 'clean virginity,' which was lauded by

the mediaeval Church as a most eminent virtue in the sight of the Lord."[14] But Schofield did not insist upon rigid adherence to a single line of correspondences. In view of the manifold significations which had been given to the pearl in previous literature,[15] this primary symbolism (virginity or chastity) may have been extended, in various parts of the poem, to include innocence in general, or even the grace of God.[16] Admittedly, too, the poet has used some of the machinery of the elegy; on the surface, the work is "openly an elegy, just as it is a dream, a debate, and a homily."[17] But fundamentally it belongs to the large body of mediaeval writings exalting "pure maidenhood." Further, this allegorical character of the poem is no mere "latent symbolism" or "emblematic result . . . perhaps reached unconsciously," as Osgood had been willing to admit, but integral and organic. The forces that release the poetic faculty, in men of great imaginative endowment, are of wider scope than the occurrences of their single lives or the movement

[14] Schofield (I), 166.
[15] Cf. Osgood, 82-83, and Schofield (II), 632-637.
[16] Schofield (I), 175; (II), 638-639.
[17] Schofield (II), 667.

f their private affections. There have been
poets, and we feel that the author of *The
Pearl* was preëminently one of these, whose
souls could be kindled by the ideal of an un-
attainable perfection.[18]

To the study of the poem Sister M. Madeleva was enabled to make a unique contri-
bution by the fact that not only is she deeply
read in the religious literature of the Middle
Ages, but also she has been for many years a
member of a religious order. So much of her
interpretation is a matter of Catholic tradition and of the inward feeling which only a
religious can fully experience that the secular critic may well hesitate to set his learning
or logic over against her intuitions. For this
reason, her vigourous and persuasive book

[18] A somewhat different non-elegiac interpretation is that
of W. K. Greene, who has argued that the poet's main intention was to illustrate the doctrine of Divine Grace; that
he employs, merely as a literary fiction, the theme of a child
lost in infancy; hence, that the dreamer and the maiden are
both to be regarded as imaginary personages created to
carry on the argument; and that it is simply the genius of a
very true poet, who happened to have an intense interest in
theological questions, which has caused us to regard them
as anything else.

The views of R. M. Garrett, who thought that the poem
conforms roughly in structure to the Mass, and that its symbolism has reference to the Eucharist, have found little support.

[xliii]

deserves, even more than do the articles pre
viously discussed, an independent reading.

Her conception of the poem has a good
deal in common with that of Schofield, who
she says, "points the way to a new and . . .
correct interpretation," but does not drive
his argument to its logical conclusions and
weakens its force by concessions to his op
ponents. Like him, she rejects utterly the
"father and daughter" theory; like him, she
finds *purity* "first and foremost the theme of
Pearl." But while the poem is to her not au
tobiographic in the literal sense of the earlier
criticism, she finds in it a much more definite
embodiment of a personal experience than
Schofield had discovered. In the disconsolate
state of the poet as revealed in the opening
section she recognizes a condition which has
been often experienced and fully described
by religious writers, especially by members
of religious orders. The natural or typical
state of young aspirants, or of those recently
entered into the religious life, is one of "in
terior sweetness or consolation." God is to
them (I am using Sister Madeleva's own lan
guage) a sensible reality, and they feel the
keenest delight in serving Him. They can

ake their meditations without difficulty
nd say their prayers without distractions.
But as a person advances in the spiritual life,
e experiences frequent withdrawals of this
ensible sweetness. The effect upon him is
nmediate. . . . He feels that God has aban-
oned him, and, left to himself, he knows
hat he can do nothing. . . . He fears that he
s failing in his pursuit of perfection and is
nore disturbed in heart and soul than he
vould be over any loss or sorrow what-
oever. This condition is known as aridity,
piritual dryness, or interior desolation."[19]
The Pearl poet, whom she finds it "almost
mpossible to regard . . . as anything but a
eligious,"[20] was experiencing an acute at-
ack of this spiritual malady. His language in
escribing it, like that of the many mystics
vhose confessions Sister Madeleva quotes, is
ymbolic. The pearl which he has lost repre-
ents the almost sensuous happiness of his
arly years as a religious; the garden-plot
vhither he repairs is not a graveyard, but
nore probably (insofar as it is not purely
ymbolic) the herb-garden of the monas-

[26] Ibid., 153-154; 178.
[27] Ibid., 191.

[xlv]

tery, associated somehow with the passin
of his spiritual joy; and the maiden who ap
pears to him in the dream is no other tha
his own soul in its potential state of per
fection. "Theologians hold that the beaut
of a human soul is so great as almost t
overpower one who should behold it in th
life."[21] Sister Madeleva protests against th
identification of the pearl lost in the garde
and the maiden, contending that, though th
dreamer speaks as if they were the same, th
maiden never refers to herself as his lo
pearl. Instead, she, "the visualization of h
soul's desired perfection,"[22] actually repri
mands him for his grief over the loss of
perishable, transitory thing, and urges hir
(stanza 62) to get for himself an endurin
pearl, such as she wears on her breast. I
other words, she rebukes him for havin
mistaken a merely natural feeling and a su
perficial enthusiasm for one of the realitie
of the spiritual life.

From this point of view, the entire dia
logue becomes "a poet's supernatural inter
course with his own soul," reminding on

[21] Ibid., 131.
[22] Ibid., 192.

strongly of such figurative presentments of
the divided self as this, by Angelo of Folig-
no:

> And I saw myself in two divisions . . . and in one divi-
> sion I saw love and every good which was God's and not
> mine, and in the other I saw myself, dry, and I saw that
> I had nothing good belonging to me.[23]

Stanza 76 of *The Pearl* might be taken as a
poet's way of saying the same thing:

> My Pearl! I am but clay unclean;
> And thou so rich and brave a rose
> Blowing where this fair bank is green
> And joy of life no fainter grows.

The language of many parts of *The Pearl* is
strikingly similar to expressions found in
mystical Catholic writings, or to turns of
speech commonly employed by all religious.
To glance at trivial matters, it is a common
practice among the religious to speak of their
lives as having begun when they took their
vows and to count their birthdays from that
time: thus, "Thou lived'st not two years in
our company."[24] Sister Madeleva has often
heard the parable of the vineyard used in innocent raillery at the expense of some mem-

[23] Algar Thorold, *Catholic Mysticism* (London, 1900),
147. Quoted by Sister Madeleva, 132.
[24] *The Pearl*, stanza 41. Cf. Sister Madeleva, 158.

ber who had entered a community late in life.[25]

From much else in her book in varying degrees illuminating or provocative, I select one further consideration, essential to her argument and in itself arresting. To a man who had taken the vow of chastity, as the Pearl poet must have done if he was an ecclesiastic, the admonitions about purity would have had a very special significance, just as the reward to which he looked forward would have been something more than the bliss common to all the righteous—a peculiar and privileged position reserved for those who have qualified themselves to be numbered among the special followers of the Lamb. In *Revelation* (xiv, 3-4) the host of the 144,000 followers of the Lamb are "they which were not defiled with women"; that is, they are "virgins" in the ancient and churchly sense of the word. Now in the poem these 144,000 followers of the Lamb are the only inhabitants of Heaven, except dignitaries like the Elders, who are shown to the dreamer; the Heaven of *The Pearl* is a Heaven of virgins. To be sure, for artistic

[25] Sister Madeleva, 166.

[xlviii]

reasons they, like the Pearl herself, are represented as maidens; but the significance of the Biblical text from which they sprang would be, to a religious, a matter of daily, almost hourly consciousness. If the dreamer were a father, whether layman or ecclesiastic, and the Pearl the soul of his virgin daughter, nothing could be more inappropriate than her exhortation to him to seek that pearl which is the special badge of virginity—the condition which he was precluded from attaining by his very relationship to her! [26] If, on the other hand, he is a discouraged young religious and she is his "own soul, as it might be in a state of perfection at this particular time of his life," [27] the plea contained in stanza 62 becomes both intelligible and poignant.

IV

This is not the place to weigh and discuss in detail these rival theories. I have tried to set them forth as objectively as possible, so that persons of different views and tastes may find here some guidance toward a satisfying reading of the poem. Fortunately, as

[26] Ibid., 153-154; 178.
[27] Ibid., 191.

[xlix]

translator I was at no point forced to choose a phrase that was definitely incompatible with any one of the different interpretations. My version presents, I think, no more and no fewer ambiguities of this sort than does the original. But lest in this essay I may unwittingly have failed to do full justice to certain opinions, it will perhaps be fairer for me to state briefly my own convictions about the meaning of the poem. The reader will then be able to allow for my prejudices and for a possible inadequacy in my statement of views with which I do not agree.

The true meaning of the poem, I think, lies along the lines of Sister Madeleva's interpretation. Its place is among the spiritual autobiographies and other mystical writings going back to Bernard of Clairvaux and Hugh of St. Victor, and including among English contemporaries of our poet Richard Rolle, Walter Hilton, Juliana of Norwich, and Thomas à Kempis. Though I find some of Sister Madeleva's parallels far-fetched, in general the resemblances between *The Pearl* and this body of literature are too striking to be accidental. As she points out,[28] if

[28] Ibid., 98.

INTRODUCTION

The Pearl were an elegy upon a little girl, it would be unique in English literature before the sixteenth century, whereas if it is an allegory of a spiritual condition it is part of a long mystical tradition which grew to a vigourous flowering in fourteenth century England. Further, I find it more satisfactory to take the Pearl-maiden as the poet's own soul in the state of its desired perfection than as an embodiment of purity in the abstract. The intimately personal tone of the poem is thus better accounted for, as well as the dreamer's reluctance to acknowledge the Pearl's right to queenly rank—an expression of his own sincere modesty in spiritual matters. In his discouraged state, he has to be *convinced* of the true preciousness of his soul. And the very first lesson he has to learn is the lesson, so congenial to mystics of all ages, that the report of the outward world which his senses give him is not to be trusted.[29]

The mysticism of *The Pearl* is somewhat hard to reconcile with the more practical and homiletic character of *Patience* and *Cleanness*, notwithstanding the passage in the lat-

[29] *The Pearl*, stanza 26. Cf. Sister Madeleva, 142.

ter[30] which uses the pearl as a symbol o
purity. Offhand one would not say that th
author of those works had much affinit
with spirits like Henry Suso, Ramon Lul
and Richard Rolle. I think that this difficult
should be faced, and that the way to mee
it is not to deny, as Sister Madeleva doe
(without any consideration of the linguisti
evidence), the common authorship of th
four poems in the Cotton manuscript. Stil
this difficulty is hardly greater for one schoc
of interpretation than for the others; ever
the proponents of the elegiac theory admi
the presence in *The Pearl* of an element o
mysticism. After all, poets, at different time
subject to different influences and seeking
to accomplish different results, bring fortl
very diverse productions. From *The Com
edy of Errors* one would scarcely predict th
Shakespeare of *The Tempest*, nor from *Ar
Evening Walk* the Wordsworth of the *Od
on Intimations of Immortality.*

But the Pearl poet was not only a mystic
he was also a theologian, or at least a mar
deeply interested in theological questions. I

[30] Lines 1110-1132. Three of the lines are quoted on p
lvi below.

[lii]

was not unnatural, therefore, that this turn of mind should show itself by the prolonged discussion of one problem of divinity on which he had meditated profoundly. In fact, the debate on the subject of heavenly recompense is relevant to the central experience of the poem in this respect: that it comforts the poet in his self-abasement by its demonstration on Scriptural authority that the Lord treats the spiritually poor like himself, who have spent but one hour in the vineyard, on equal terms with the fortunate, who laboured throughout the day.[31]

There remains, however, a possible objection to Sister Madeleva's interpretation which I think she has not removed and which, I confess, I am not altogether sure how to meet. It is easy to understand the poet's insistence, through the mouth of the maiden, that the 144,000 followers of the Lamb share an equal and communal bliss; but why should he extend the principle of equality, as he does, to *all* the righteous—even setting himself in opposition, on this point, to the theological guides he usually followed? If there is an exclusive and peculiar position in

[31] Sister Madeleva, 165.

the Kingdom reserved for virgins, what becomes of the principle of equality, so earnestly enforced throughout the central section of the poem? Or why, in a poem setting forth the hopes of a religious for a quite special kind of bliss in Heaven, should we find an elaborate exposition of the doctrine that there is no hierarchy among the redeemed? Note especially the uncompromising pronouncement in stanza 51:

> For there the same is each man's prize.

To raise the question, perhaps, is merely to betray my own inexperience of casuistry; but it is the sort of puzzle that naturally occurs to the lay mind, and it has not received an answer. For myself, though I accept Sister Madeleva's main line of argument, I must hold that in many parts of the debate the poet was thinking of purity in the sense in which it may be attained, or striven for, by all, not exclusively by the celibate—thinking, shall we say, of the pure *in heart*. And I would call attention to one rather surprising choice of a word. It occurs at what Sister Madeleva justly calls "the climactic moment of the entire poem,"[32] when the maiden ex-

[32] Stanza 62. Cf. Sister Madeleva, 172.

ains why Jesus likened the pearl of price
the Kingdom of Heaven:

> For endless round, and full of mirth,
> Flawless, it is, and pure, and clear,
> In fee by the *righteous* held henceforth.
> Lo! on my breast that pearl I bear.

ow it will be remembered that, through-
t the section immediately preceding, the
jective "righteous" was used consistently
contrast with "innocent"—the former re-
rring to men who, after sin and repentance,
e virtuously; the latter, to those without
. In the third line quoted above, we might
ve expected "innocent" or "clean" if the
plication is to those only who have taken
e vow of chastity. Instead we have "right-
us." In interpreting the poem I would not
t too much stress upon a single line or
ord, but it seems to me that this is not the
ly instance in which the poet has deliber-
ely caused the symbolism of the pearl to
ke on its wider meaning. In *Cleanness* the
earl is made the symbol of a *restored* pur-
y, a purity which may be attained through
pentance:

THE PEARL

How canst thou come to His country save thou be
clean? . . .
Thou mayst shine through shrift, though thou hast
served shame,
And purify thee with penance, till thou be a pearl.

We remember that in *The Pearl* there is ;
allusion to Jacob, who was assuredly no vi
gin, as among those graciously welcomed
the Kingdom. While the poem, then, m;
have had a peculiar and private significan
to its author, as it has to religious to-day, l
has given to his doctrine of purity a broad'
human and not merely an esoteric impor
Like so many other allegorical composition
however, *The Pearl* attains its wider mear
ing at some sacrifice of coherence and co
sistency.

Perhaps this is no more than to concede
point already elaborated by Professor J. l
Fletcher in an excellent essay on the poer
which appeared some years earlier than Si
ter Madeleva's book. The mediaeval prac
tice, he argues, of positing or assuming
multiplicity of reference for any given syn
bol, of which the familiar "fourfold sense
of Dante's great work is only one instanc
makes it probable that *The Pearl* had a nun
ber of significances, all equally valid. ";

…edieval symbol of this kind is like a crystal
f many facets." He would even admit that
the child in question may have really lived
…d died," "may have been the poet's own
…aughter."[33] Fletcher's argument does not,
…r me, dispose of the objections to this par-
…cular hypothesis which Sister Madeleva has
…ormulated, but it does call attention to an
…mportant and too often ignored aspect of
…ost mediaeval productions of an allegorical
…ast.

V

From these highly abstract matters I turn
…bruptly to certain aspects of poetic form,
…ne description of which at least will not lack
…oncreteness. *The Pearl* contains one hun-
…red and one stanzas, arranged in twenty
…roups, each group (with one exception)
…ontaining five stanzas. Presumably, the poet
…ntended that there should be exactly one
…undred stanzas,[34] for one hundred was the
…erfect number—there are one hundred can-
…os in the three parts of the *Divine Comedy*.
…Vithin each group the five stanzas are joined

[33] Fletcher, 20-21.
[34] The XVth is the section with the extra stanza. Possibly
…anza 72, after being marked for rejection, was included
…rough a later inadvertence on the part of poet or copyist.

by a link—a word or phrase which appea
in each opening half-line (after the first sta
za) and as a refrain (sometimes varied sligh
ly) in the final position of each last line. Th
link is used again in the first line of the ne
section; thus each successive section is tie
to the preceding, as within the sections th
stanzas are tied each to each. The final sec
tion, moreover, takes its link from the oper
ing line of the poem, the verbal echo her
being accompanied by a subtle evocation c
thought and feeling. This complicated sys
tem may be more readily understood b
glancing at the present version, in which
have reproduced it — with slight modifica
tions here and there. (For instance, Sectio
V, which is regular, will show the norm.)

The verse is of four beats, and its genera
movement is iambic. Recent textual studies,
demonstrating the many errors in a ver
corrupt manuscript, have tended to show
that the poet's lines were metrically mor
regular than was formerly thought. Still, i
the occasional lines containing several extr
syllables we see some influence upon hin
here of the looser measure of that Old Eng

---

[35] By Gollancz and Emerson.

lish prosody which the poets of the North
and West had revived and which he himself
used in other works. As is uniformly the case
in the latter, a very large number of the lines
of *The Pearl* have alliteration.

The stanza is of twelve lines, rhyming
ababababbcbc. The balance of the two parts,
octave and quatrain, gives an effect somewhat similar to that of the Petrarchan son-
net. Both rhyme-scheme and stanza-linking,
however, are of the late Middle Ages. Link-
ing through alliteration alone (of stanza to
stanza, or of lines within a stanza) was a device common to a whole group of Northern
Middle English poems, of which *Sir Perceval*
is the best known; it had been used even earlier in certain songs, and is probably of pop-
ular origin. But the variety of "enchaining"
or "*rime concatenée*" employed in *The Pearl*,
which carries over a *refrain* to the opening
and repeats it in the closing line of a stanza,
was apparently influenced by Romance or
mediaeval Latin models.[36] Undoubtedly the
exigencies of a rhyme-scheme so complex
frequently forced the poet to employ words
in unusual meanings, and gives to his verse

[36] Cf. Medary, 264-265, 270.

at times the appearance of something rather strained and laboured. Nevertheless, the poem with its many repetitive elements, often delicately varied, enchants the ear. "*The Pearl*," writes Professor Saintsbury,[37] "is a sort of *carillon*—not indeed of joyful but of melancholy sweetness—a tangle, yet in no disorder, of symphonic sound, running and interlacing itself with an ineffable deliciousness."

The following version of the poem will be found to be reasonably close to the original.[38] Metre, of course, and even more rhyme, force the translator into continual slight liberties with his text; but I venture to think that such departures from literalness are more than compensated for by some likeness in general effect, which, in the case of *The Pearl*, can be obtained only through rhymed verse. While employing the rhyme-scheme and the stanza-linking, I have not attempted to reproduce the alliteration of the original—at least, not with any exact

[37] *History of English Prosody* (London, 1906), I, 109.

[38] Emendations of the text accepted for the purposes of this rendering may be consulted in the Bowdoin Edition. I have not followed the readings of that edition in every instance, however.

[lx]

correspondence. Rather, I have permitted alliterative effects where these could be had naturally and without straining. As far as possible, I have avoided archaisms and words worn thin by excessive use in romantic poetry. In short, I have sought to put the poem into a form which, while faithful to the original, shall keep as much as possible of the vigour and freshness of the Middle English, without too much disturbing the modern reader by its strangeness.

VI

For all its elaborateness of technique and its infusion with a type of mystical experience to most persons unaccustomed and to many uncongenial, the poem has an extraordinary vitality. Though some of its implications may be apprehended only by the few, the depth and sincerity of its feeling, and a certain fineness of spiritual texture in the author, can be mistaken by none. Many of his personal and artistic traits have appeared clearly enough in the foregoing analysis: conjoined with his mystical tendency, his typically mediaeval fondness for dialectic; his architectonic skill; his scrupulous con-

science; his humility; the courtly grace of
his address. When I try to think whom he
most resembles among later English poets, I
find that certain of the seventeenth century
group come first to mind, especially George
Herbert and Vaughn and Crashaw. Indeed
The Pearl is a "metaphysical" poem in the
broad sense in which, according to Professor
Grierson, all poetry may be so described
which "has been inspired by a philosophical
conception of the universe and the rôle as-
signed to the human spirit in the great drama
of existence." But now and again, especially
when he turns to the outward world, the author of *The Pearl* puts us in mind of poets
even nearer to us than that seventeenth century group. Much of his description, of
course, when not symbolic, is merely deco-
rative—the conventionalized trees and flowers and birds of the mediaeval earthly paradise. Yet how frequently he delights us by a
line that attests his own delicate responsive-
ness to the sights and sounds of the country-
side—by some glimpse of a pleasant English
lawn such as Tennyson was to know; or by
the murmur of a brook conveyed to us in
words whose music suggests the sensitive ear

INTRODUCTION

of Keats; or then by some turn of speech as homespun and familiar as a phrase of Wordsworth; or by a picture of winter stars, shining steadily in the still night, that could have come from Coleridge at his happiest. But these are not the gifts for which he would have wished his work to be chiefly valued; nor should we allow such chance resemblances to one or another later writer to blur our final impression of the distinct individuality of a sincere and rare human being, who in his own right was a distinguished poet.

THE PEARL

THE PEARL

I

I

PEARL, for prince's pleasure fit,
  Set clean in gold to make him mirth! . . .
One pearl there was, my favourite,
So round, so smooth, so small of girth,—
From Orient none so exquisite;
And wheresoever, south or north,
On jewels gay I set my wit,
I held my pearl unmatched in worth.
   Alas! I lost it in the earth;
   Through grass it slipped in garden-plot.
   Love took my joy and left me dearth.
   I mourn that pearl without a spot.

2

Since from me in that spot it sprung,
Bereft I grieve for the past delight
Which once could cancel all my wrong
And raise my good to greater height.
Now thick on heart sharp sorrows throng,
Breast swells and burns both day and night;
Yet sweet, in one still hour, the song
That stole to me and eased my plight.
  Forsooth came many a thought and sight,
  How stained its beauty now with clot.
  O earth, thou marr'st a jewel white,
  The pearl, my own, without a spot.

THE PEARL

3

Sweet herbs around that spot will spread,
Such riches there lie mouldering,
And blossoms yellow and blue and red
Their glory to the sunlight fling,
Nor flower nor fruit be witherëd
Above that place where dark roots cling;
For save the grain in earth lie dead,
No wheat were won for harvesting.
   Sure, born of good is each good thing;
   Where seed so fair has run to rot,
   Fair spices in that place will spring
   From the pearl, my own, without a spot.

4

Toward that spot of earth whereon
I speak, I walked through garden-green,
In August in a high season,
When grain is cut with sickles keen.
There, on the bank my pearl rolled down,
Pleasant herbs made shade and screen,
Gillyflower, ginger, and gromillon,
And peonies powdered in between.
  If all was fair that eyes had seen,
  Sweet too the odour from that plot,
  Where worthily now dwells, I ween,
  My precious pearl without a spot.

THE PEARL

5

Before that spot, with hands clasped tight,
A freezing care my breast around,
I stood, my heart in pain despite
All ways to peace that reason found.
With fighting thoughts and fearful sleight,
I mourned my pearl there sunk in ground;
Though Christ with comfort did invite,
My tortured will fast held me bound.
  I dropped upon the flowery mound;
  Such fragrance to my senses shot,
  I fell in slumber-dream profound—
  Of that precious pearl without a spot.

THE PEARL

II

6

FROM that spot my soul leaped free in s
 The while in trance my body lies;
My spirit's borne, by His dear grace,
To regions far of high emprise.
I knew not where that country was
In all the world, nor whence should rise
Those cliffs aglow from top to base,
The woods, the rocks, that met my eyes.
  No one e'er wove in tapestries
  Such gleaming glory as was there,
  Nor ever wrought with brilliant dyes
  Adornment half so gay and rare!

THE PEARL

Adorned on every side that ground
With crystal cliffs; the trees that grew
In woods thereunder and around,
Both bole and branch, were India-blue,
Each trunk with spreading ramage crowned,
The foliage silver, burnished new,
That shimmered when some gleam had found
Its way the leafy branches through.
   The gravel that the shores did strew,
   Of orient pearls it was, I think,
   That shone as never sunbeams do,—
   Such the adornment of the brink.

8

The adornments of that fair demesne
Made me forget to grieve and gird;
So fresh the fruits, their scent, I ween,
As food, renewëd strength conferred.
And small and great, the trees between,
Of flaming plumage many a bird
Flew hither and yon; such joyance keen
Citole or cithern never stirred.
    With voices in a sweet accord,
        They beat their wings and sang full clear
        Commingled thus the seen and heard
        Adornments both for eye and ear.

THE PEARL

Adorned that wood in fairest guise
Where Fortune leads me, now restored;
The power to tell its qualities
No skill in language would afford.
Still on I walk in happy wise,
Without annoy or step untoward,
And ever the farther, fairer rise
The plants, the spice, the trees, the sward,
And hedges, meadows, river-bord
Steep-sloping, bright as thread-of-gold.
To the water's edge I wandered—Lord!
Fair that adornment to behold!

THE PEARL

10

The adornments of the brook, outspread,
Were radiant banks of beryl bright;
Swiftly, with sound low murmurëd,
The water rushed in its course aright.
The stones that lay in the water's bed,
Like glass in sun their points of white,
Or streaming stars high overhead —
All men asleep through winter night.
   For every pebble within my sight
   Was emerald, sapphire, precious stone;
   The pools were all agleam with light
   From these adornments of their own.

THE PEARL

III

11

THOSE rich adornments of champaign,
  Of wood and water, dale and hill,
Brought blessëd joy, assuaged my pain,
Cured my distress and all my ill.
With blissful heart and busy brain
  turned along a hurrying rill;
The more I trod that watery plain,
The stronger joy my heart did fill.
  For Fortune hath her own way still,
  Send she solace or trial sore,
  And he to whom she shows goodwill
  Aspires ever to more and more.

12

More the weal in such a wise
Than I could tell though long I stayed,
For earthly heart cannot surmise
One tenth my joy from grove and glade.
Wherefore I thought that Paradise
Across those banks stood fair arrayed—
The water but a gay device,
'Twixt mirth and mirth a boundary laid.
  The castle-walls, by slope or shade,
  I fancied hid on yonder shore;
  But stream so deep I dared not wade,
  And longing grew still more and more.

THE PEARL

More and more, that distant lea
Across the brook my longing drew.
Though all was fair surrounding me,
The far-off land more fair I knew.
I scanned the ground, moved stumblingly;
Of ford I sought some sign or clue;
But more there was of jeopardy
Ahead than here in closer view.
    No woe, I thought, that might ensue
    Should make me falter or give o'er
    My quest. . . . Then saw I something new,
    That stirred my mind still more and more.

14

More marvels were to daunt my sight.
I saw, beyond that pleasant mere,
A crystal cliff, reflecting light
Of rays that danced and leaped in air.
Below, there sat a maiden bright
Of gentle mien, none worthier,
Her garments all of dazzling white—
She was no stranger; I knew her.
   Like gold-thread of embroiderer,
   Her beauty gleamed against that shore,
   While still I looked with mind astir
   Longer, and knew her more and more.

THE PEARL

The more her beauteous form and face
I scanned with lively look intent,
There came such gladdening glory and grace
As seldom before to me was sent.
I wished to call, but shamefastness
With stab at heart would still prevent;
I saw her in so strange a place,
Well might the blow be violent.
    Toward me her lovely brow she bent
    And face, as ivory smooth. It tore
    My heart, and deep bewilderment
    Grew, ever the longer, more and more.

THE PEARL

IV

16

MORE than desire, my fear rose high,
Stock-still I stood, and dared not call;
With mouth tight shut and open eye,
I stood as quiet as hawk in hall.
A ghostly meaning, truthfully,
I guessed, but feared what might befall,—
Lest she elude me ere that I
Could find my voice effectual.
  Still gracious, comely, smooth and small,
  She rises now, that slender maid,
  Assumes her royal state withal,
  A precious thing in pearls arrayed.

THE PEARL

17

Those royal pearls arrayed in the sun
To see, men would a grace esteem.
As fleur-de-lys fresh, that goodly one
Came down the bank across the stream.
Glistening white her mantle shone,
Open at the sides; and ne'er, I deem,
Were merrier pearls to look upon
Than those that bordered hem and seam.
  And double rows of pearls agleam
  The loosely flowing folds displayed;
  Her kirtle like her robe did seem,
  Its edges too with pearls arrayed.

18

With pearls arrayed (for I beheld
No jewel else) a crown she bore
Of mother-of-pearl, high pinnacled,
Inwrought with many a figured flower.
No band her circling hair withheld,
No covering on her head she wore.
Her face the ivory's white excelled,
But serious as a grave seignior.
    The hair that fell her shoulders o'er
    Was like bright gold thus loosely laid;
    Her collar deep nor lacking store
    Of pearls in broidered rows arrayed.

THE PEARL

Arrayed and sewed was every hem,
At hands, at sides, at aperture,
With whitest pearls—no other gem
On raiment dazzling white. And sure,
Unblemished 'twas, a pearl supreme,
That on her breast was set secure;
And who would judge its worth, to them
The essay would bring discomfiture!
    For tongue could not itself inure
    To speech so delicately made
    As it was clean and clear and pure,
    The pearl there in the midst arrayed.

THE PEARL

Arrayed in garments white, each piece,
Across from me she approached the bourne.
No gladder man from here to Greece
Than I who saw her thither turn!
She was nearer to me than aunt or niece;
The higher, so, was my joy upborne,
When she tendered speech, with low curtsie:
In gentle woman's way time-worn,
    Removed the crown that did adorn
    Her head, and joyful welcome made.
    O, well for me that I was born,
    To answer her in pearls arrayed!

THE PEARL

V

21

O PEARL, arrayed in pearls of white,
  Art thou the pearl I sorrowed for,
Weeping," I said, "alone by night,
By day my wound but covering o'er,
Since in the grass thou slid'st from sight?
I, sad and spent, am tortured sore,
Whilst thou art come to all delight
By Paradise' untroubled shore.
  What fate my jewel hither bore,
  And left me there, grief's prisoner?
  For since us two apart it tore,
  I have been a joyless jeweller."

22

The jewel who in pearls was dressed
Did lift her face, with eyes of grey,
Again with orient crown invest
Herself, and seriously say:
"Fair sir, thou misinterpretest
To think thy pearl is done away,
That is enclosed within a chest
So comely as this garden gay—
   Forever here to live and play,
   Where loss and mourning never were:
   A treasure-chest for thee, in fay,
   Wert thou a gentle jeweller.

THE PEARL

23

'But, jeweller, if thy joy thou lose
For a gem, though dear, it seems to me
Quite far astray thy reason goes
On matter of such transiency.
What thou didst lose was but a rose,
That flowered and withered naturally.
The coffer that did thy pearl enclose
Has proved it pearl of price to be.
 Thy fate 'from naught made aught' for thee;
 To call him thief is but to err.
 Of ill thou blam'st the remedy!
 Ungrateful art thou, jeweller."

24

A jewel to me was this guest,
Her sayings jewels were to prove.
"In truth," said I, "my blissful best,
My ill thou cur'st. May it behoove
Thee pardon me, for I had guessed
Fate did my pearl from life remove.
'Tis found! I'll live with it, and rest
Me merry in this sunny grove,
    And praise my Lord His laws, Whose lov
    To such great bliss hath brought me near.
    This stream but crossed, on shore thereof
    Were I a joyful jeweller!"

THE PEARL

"Jeweller," said that innocent,
"Why jest ye men, so mad ye be?
Three words at once from thy tongue went,
And unadvisëd were all three.
Thou know'st not what one of them meant;
Thy words before thy wits did flee.
Thou say'st that I am resident
Just here because thine eyes me see;
    That thou thyself here, secondly,
    Shalt live with me, thou dost infer;
    Thirdly, to cross this stream scot-free
    Is not for joyful jeweller.

THE PEARL

"I GIVE that jeweller little praise
    Who trusts all that he sees with eye,
And right and courtesy he gainsays
Who thinks our Lord would make a lie,—
Our Lord Who promised your life to raise,
Though Fortune made your flesh to die.
Ye set His words contrary-ways
Believing but what ye espy.
    Of pride is this a quality
    That doth a good man ill befit:
    On no averment to rely
    Save his own reason judge of it.

27

"Now judge thy words, how light and vain
As speech that man to God should owe.
Thou say'st thou'lt live in this domain:
Thou mightst ask leave,—and even so
The boon thou still mightst fail to gain.
This water thou wouldst cross: but know,
To counsel new thou must attain;
Thy corse must cold in earth sink low;
    'Twas damned where Eden's trees did grow;
    Our forefather turned it to dross.
    Through dreary death must each man go,
    Ere judgéd fit this stream to cross."

28

"If now thy judgement, sweet," I said,
"Renews my grief, then I despair.
The lost that is recoverëd
Must I forego while life shall wear?
Why must it be now come, now sped?
Great pain my Pearl gives me to bear.
What use serves treasure but, once fled,
To bring men bitter tears and care?
    If in my Pearl I have no share,
    I mind not though I droop, nor yet
    From home be driven how far so e'er!
    Save grief, what judge men they shall get.

THE PEARL

29

"Thou judgest, nothing but distress
And pain," she said. "Why dost thou so?
From din of grief o'er losses less,
The larger gain men oft forgo.
Thou shouldst thee better rule and bless,
And love thy God, in weal, in woe,
For anger wins thee not a cress;
Who needs must bear, less wild should grow.
    For dance thou mayst as any doe,
    And thrash and toss, and raging chide;
    When thou canst no further, to nor fro,
    His judgement then thou must abide.

30

"The Lord shall judge; He shall bestow;
Nor swerve one foot from path He shall.
Thy amends are not of worth an O,
Though sorrow ever with thee dwell.
Seek His compassion, be not slow,
Leave thy dispute, cease to rebel;
Thy prayer may move His pity so,
And Mercy then her powers may tell.
  His comfort may the grief dispel,
  The losses that thy spirit dim,
  For marred or made, or sore or well,
  To ordain and judge doth lie with Him."

THE PEARL

VII

31

HER judgement then acknowledging,
  I said, "Not angry be my Lord
If headstrong, hasty words I fling,
My heart with grief so cut and scored.
I seek His mercy, as at spring
Whence welling water is outpoured.
Astray, rebuke me not with sting
Of cruel speech, my dear adored,
  But comfort me with soothing word,
  Remembering with pity this:
  'Twixt Care and me *thou* mad'st accord,
  Who wert the ground of all my bliss.

32

"My bliss, my grief—both these thou wert,
But more the grief. From that time on,
When thou didst pass beyond all hurt,
I knew not where my pearl was gone.
Again to see it dulls the smart,
When we took leave, we were at one;
That wroth we now be, God avert,—
We meet so seldom by stock or stone.
   Thou speakest courtesy; I know none;
   I am but clay, and much remiss;
   Mercy of Christ, Mary, and John—
   There is the ground of all my bliss.

THE PEARL

"Thee joyous in thy bliss I see;
A man, I, mournful, desolate,—
Scant heed thereto I mark in thee,
Although my griefs be hot and great.
But in thy presence now my plea
Is this: that we two cease debate,
And that thou tell me soberly
What life thou lead'st early and late.
   For I am glad that thy estate
   Such honour has, and happiness;
   It is my highway fortunate
   Of joy, and ground of all my bliss."

THE PEARL

34

"May bliss attend thee, sir, I pray,"
Said she, her beauty shining clear.
"Be welcome here to walk and stay;
Thy speech now brings me right good cheer
High pride and overbearing way,
I promise thee, are hateful here.
My Lord loves chiding not, for they
Are meek who live His presence near.
    When in His place thou shalt appear,
    Be thine devout humility;
    My Lord the Lamb doth hold it dear,
    And ground of all my bliss is He.

THE PEARL

35

'A blissful life thou say'st I lead,
And thou wouldst learn its circumstance.
I was of tender age (no need
To tell thee) when thy pearl went thence.
But my Lord the Lamb took me indeed
In marriage, by His sufferance,
Crowned me as queen, in bliss to speed
For length of days' continuance,
    Endowed with His inheritance
    His dear one: I am His alone;
    His lineage, praise, and excellence
    The root and ground of bliss I own."

VIII

36

"BLISSFUL," said I, "can this be true—
And else forgive me that I spake—
Art thou the queen of heavens blue,
Honoured where'er sun's light doth break?
From Mary's virgin flower there grew
A Child, and grace did there awake.
Must not some greater worth endue
One who from her the crown would take?
 And for her matchless sweetness' sake
 We call her Phoenix of Araby,
 After that bird of spotless make,
 Like to the Queen of Courtesy."

37

"Courteous Queen!"—as suppliant would,
She knelt to ground and veiled her face—
"Pattern of Mother- and Maidenhood!
Blessëd Beginner of every grace!"
Rising, a while she silent stood,
Then said to me, "Of those who chase
And seize their prey a multitude,
But usurpers none, are within this place.
  That Empress's domains embrace
  Earth, Heaven, Hell; and yet will she
  None disinherit or abase,
  For she is Queen of Courtesy.

38

"The Kingdom's Court where God's Self i
This nature has in its very frame:
That every one who gains ingress
Is queen or king in deed and name
Of all the realm; none dispossess
The others, but their wealth acclaim;
And each would wish (vain such access!)
The others' crowns worth five the same.
   But my Lady, from whom Jesus came,
   High over all hath empery,
   Nor any here account it blame,
   For she is Queen of Courtesy.

THE PEARL

In courtesy, as saith Saint Paul,
Of Jesus Christ we members are.
As head and navel, arms, legs—all
One person serve, one body share,
Each Christian soul is spiritual
Limb of the gracious Lord. Compare
Thy human frame: is hate or gall
Of part 'gainst part felt anywhere?
    Thine arm, or finger, ring may wear,
    Nor head thereat resentful be;
    And such the joyful love we bear
    Toward King and Queen, in courtesy."

THE PEARL

40

"The courtesy that doth obtain,
And charity, your host among
I grant," I said, "but, speaking plain,
I see not how it can belong
To Heaven's justice thou shouldst reign
As queen so high, who wert so young.
What greater worship could he gain
That had endured the harsh world's wrong
    And penance borne in anguish strong
    Through years, to win felicity?
    How honoured more than in such throng
    To be crowned as king in courtesy?

THE PEARL

IX

41

T HAT courtesy, if thou speak'st true,
   Dear maiden, is by far too free.
Thou never learned'st (for not quite two,
The years thou lived'st in our company)
To pray or praise, nor yet go through
Thy Creed or Pater; and to be,
The first day, queen! I'll not allow
That God would act so wrongfully.
   'Twould well befit thy quality
   If thou in Heaven as countess sat,
   Or lady lower in degree,
   But queen!—it is not time for that!"

42

"Nor term nor time may Him compel,"
She said, "in Whom is goodness stored.
He can do naught but fair and well;
All His decrees with truth accord.
As Matthew in your Mass doth tell,
In the faithful gospel of God's Word,
A closely fitted parable
Doth image of high Heaven afford.
  'My Kingdom is like unto a lord,'
  He saith, 'who did a vineyard own.
  The yearly labour now was toward,
  The time was come when vines were gro

THE PEARL

' 'That time of year the labourer knows.
And so, to hire for daily fee
His workmen, early the lord arose,
And some he found. They all agree
For a penny a day, those whom he chose,
And set forth with great industry,
And hard they toil in the vineyard's rows,
Cut, twine, and bind all tidily.
   Toward noon, at the market-place is he,
   And sees, there standing, idle men.
   "Why stand ye idle?" he says. "Think ye
   That time this day is endless, then?"

44

"'"Ere time of dawn, till sun was high,"
Together thus they spoke their thought,
"Here have we stood, this market by,
And still to work are bidden not."
"Into my vineyard! Go and try
What ye can!"—he gave the pledge they so
"All reasonable wages I
Will pay, come night, as true man ought."
    Among the vines they came, and wrough
    Meanwhile the lord went on his way,
    And new men to the vineyard brought
    At times. . . . Far gone the precious day.

THE PEARL

45

" 'At time of day of evensong,
Last hour of sun's now sinking fire,
He sees there idle fellows strong,
And gravely of them doth inquire,
"Why stand ye idle, days so long?"
Their work, they said, had yet no buyer.
"Go work my vineyard, yeomen young,
Do what ye can till light expire."
  Straightway upon the world entire
  Darkness fell; there was no sun.
  He summoned them to take their hire;
  The time was spent, and day was done.

THE PEARL

X

46

"'THAT the time was past the lord did kno[w]
And called the reeve: "Sir, pay these me[n]
Give them the wages that I owe;
And that none reproach me, I am fain
Thou set them in a single row,
And a penny give to every swain;
Begin with the last, where they stand low,
Till to the first thou dost attain."
    The first began then to complain,
    And said that they had laboured sore:
    "These but one hour have borne the strain[,]
    It seems we ought to get the more.

THE PEARL

47

" ' "Yea, us, we think, more one should owe,
By sun's heat through long hours attacked,
Than these who worked for barely two;
Thou mak'st all equal by this act."
Then the lord, to one who argued so:
"Friend, from thy wage I'll not subtract
A mite. Take that thine is, and go.
'A penny the stint' was our compact.
    Why now demur? Didst not contract
    For a penny a day with me, before?
    More than a covenant's terms exact
    One may not claim. Why ask for more?

THE PEARL

48

" ' "Nay more: may I not do whate'er
I will with mine own, the small and great?
Or doth thine eye with evil stare
Because I am good and none do cheat?"
"Thus I," said Christ, "the award declare:
The last shall be first within the gate;
The first, though swift, the last; for there
Are many called, few designate." '

Thus always, come they ne'er so late,
Or lowly be, are served the poor;
Of all their toil though brief the date,
God's mercy is by far the more.

the poor

49

"Mine here more joy and bliss have been,
Life's bloom, and ladyship beside,
Than all the folk on earth could win,
Should they their mere deserts abide.
Although I did but now begin,—
To the vineyard came at eventide,—
No sooner stepped I herewithin,
The Lord my reckoning satisfied.
    Yet others, who more time applied,
    Who moiled and sweated long, of yore,
    Their wages still have been denied—
    Perchance may be a full year more."

THE PEARL

50

Then more outright I spoke to her:
"Unreasonable thine argument;
As fable, Holy Writ would err
If so His justice could be bent.
These plain, conclusive words occur
In Psalter of Old Testament:
'Thou rewardest every man after
His work, High King, fore-ordinant.'
    If they to thee thy wage present
    Ere his to him who day's heat bore,
    Then larger meed has smaller stent.
    Pay still grows less as toil is more!"

THE PEARL

XI

51

"TWIXT more and less no difference lies,"
    She said, "within His realm's frontier,
For there the same is each man's prize,
Howso great or small his worth appear.
Our gentle Chief no niggard is,
Whether mild His dealing or severe—
Gifts poured, as streams when runnels rise;
From deeps exhaustless, waters clear.
    Large franchise theirs who stood in fear
    Toward Him Who gives in every proof
    Succour from sin,—no bliss too dear,
    For the grace of God is great enough.

52

"But now thou urgest, countering me,
That wrongly was my penny ta'en,—
Too large a wage, since tardily
I went to work, thou say'st again.
What holy man of prayer is he
(Came ever one within thy ken?)
That did not forfeit heavenly fee
By deeds he did, somehow, somewhen?
   And old, the oftener these men
    Wrought evil, kept from good aloof;
   Mercy and grace must pilot then,
    For the grace of God is great enough.

THE PEARL

53

But the innocent, enough their sum
Of grace; they all at birth descend
Into baptismal water—come
Then to the vineyard. . . . Signs impend
That day to night will soon succumb;
Shadows in sky death's dark portend.
The Lord then gives their premium
To servants who did not offend.
  They were there, they did His will attend;
  Why should He not their score clear off?
  Yes, pay them at the first day's end?
  For the grace of God is great enough.

54

"Known well enough 'tis, made was man
For perfect bliss and infinite;
Which forfeit was, and woe began,
When Adam did an apple bite.
By that one meal we incurred the ban
To die in grief, far from delight,
And then to dwell for endless span
In Hell's fierce heat, without respite.
    But help soon reached us in that plight,
    When rich blood ran on rood so rough,
    And precious water, flowing white;
    The grace of God welled great enough.

55

Enough from out that source did well,
Blood and water from the broad wound;
The blood bought us from hurt of Hell,
And from the second death unbound;
Baptism, the water, sooth to tell,
That flows from spear so grimly ground,
Cleanses the sins unbearable
Wherewith in death us Adam drowned.
  Each bar to bliss, the whole world round,
  Is now withdrawn, for our behoof;
  In happy hour, true weal re-found;
  And the grace of God is great enough.

XII

56

"GRACE enough the man may have
Who sins anew, if he repent,
With grief and sighs forgiveness crave,
And bear his pain as penitent.
But unerring right and reason save
Evermore all the innocent;
For God the judgement never gave
That guiltless souls have punishment.
  To grace, if Mercy's aid be lent,
  The guilty may be brought, contrite;
  But one to evil never bent,
  The innocent, is saved by right.

THE PEARL

57

"Salvation won by right or grace,
Either, does reason's law fulfil;
The righteous man shall see His face,
The guileless know His domicile.
The Psalmist says of just this case:
'Lord, who shall climb to Thy high hill,
Or rest within Thy holy place?'
Himself the answer render will:
    'Who with his hands hath done no ill,
    His heart who keepeth pure and bright,
    His foot in firm place standeth still.'
    The innocent is saved by right.

✗

58

"The righteous man no less shall gain;
He shall approach that noble pile
Who doth not take his life in vain
Or harm his neighbour by some wile.
Our King, as Solomon saw plain,
Received one such with gracious smile,
Who had been shown his Lord's domain
In the straitened years of his exile,
    As who should say, 'Lo, yon fair isle!
    Be thou but brave, all in thy sight
    Is thine to win.'—Secure the while,
    The innocent is safe by right.

THE PEARL

59

'Anent the righteous, David's thought
Leans somewhat to the other side:
'To judgement bring Thy servant not;
Before Thee none are justified.'
So, when to that Court thou art brought
Where all our causes shall be cried,
Do thou renounce thy right to aught,
On grounds by this same text supplied.
    But He on bloody cross that died,
    His blessëd hands transpiercëd quite,
    Give thee to pass, when thou art tried,
    By innocence and not by right.

here

60

"Who reads aright, learn from the Book
Which followers of Jesus made
How, when His earthly way He took,
Folk brought to Him their bairns for aid,—
For healing of His touch and look
His blessing on their children prayed.
The twelve disciples, by rebuke
And protest, would the crowd dissuade.
  'Suffer the children,' He sweetly said,
  'To come to Me, nor them affright.
  For such, the Kingdom stands arrayed.'
  The innocent are saved by right.

THE PEARL

H IS meek disciples then, by name,
   He called, and of the Kingdom taught,
How, save as a little child one came,
One should of it inherit naught.
The stainless, truthful, free from blame,
Who spot nor speck of sin have caught,
But knock, and men unbolt for them,
And entrance give as soon as sought.
   There is the bliss the jeweller thought
   To find in gems; who sold, 'tis said,
   His linen, wool, and all, and bought
   Therefor a pearl unblemishëd.

THE PEARL

" 'The unblemished pearl, for whose great w
He gave his all, that jeweller,'
So said the Father of sea and earth,
'Is like the Realm of Heaven's sphere.'
For endless round, and full of mirth,
Flawless, it is, and pure, and clear,
In fee by the righteous held henceforth.
Lo! on my breast that pearl I bear.
   In sign of peace He set it there,
   My Lord the Lamb, Whose blood was she
   Do *thou* the frantic world forswear,
   And buy thy pearl unblemishëd."

THE PEARL

63

"Unblemished Pearl, in purity
That bear'st," I said, "the pearl of price,
Who formed thy figure? Wise was he
Who wrought thy weeds with craft so nice.
Of Nature's make thou canst not be;
Never Pygmalion's hand precise
Could limn thy face; nor philosophy
Of Aristotle, thy properties—
 Thy hue more fair than fleur-de-lys,
 Thy gracious bearing, Heaven-bred.
 Tell me, Shining, what virtue is
 In that thy pearl unblemishëd?"

THE PEARL

64

"The unblemished Lamb, my Destiny
So dear," she said, "Who all things could,
Chose me for mate,—howso it be
That strange, erstwhile, such marriage would
Have seemed. When I left your watery
Dark world, He called me to His good:
'Come hither to Me, my love; in thee
There is no spot'; on the dais stood
    And washed my robes in His own blood,
    And crowned me pure in maidenhead;
    With strength and beauty me endowed
    And clad in pearls unblemishëd."

THE PEARL

'Unblemished bride, in splendour come
With regal emblems girt about,
What kind of being is that Lamb
Who thee for wife would single out?
To attain such ladyship, one clomb
High over others, past all doubt,
Who bore for Christ long martyrdom—
The comeliest of His devout.
   Yet thou those worthy ones didst rout,
   Thyself to Him as bride wert led,
   So strong thou wert, of heart so stout,
   A matchless maid, unblemishëd!''

XIV

66

"UNBLEMISHED," said she, "by least b
So much with right may be professed;
But 'matchless queen'—that said I not,
Which thou to me attributest.
Wives of the Lamb, we, without spot,
A hundred and forty thousand blest,
As in Apocalypse, I wot,
To John the Saint was manifest.
   On Sion Hill's delightful crest
   The Apostle saw, in ghostly dream,
   That host in wedding raiment dressed,
   In the city New Jerusalem.

THE PEARL

"With Jerusalem this has to do: —
Would thou His nature know," she said,
"(My Lamb, my Lord, my Jewel true,
My Bliss, my Love, my Joy's one Head!),
Pitifully Isaiah drew
His gentle sweetness, where 'tis read
How men the Glorious Guiltless slew,
Though nothing ill He merited:
  'As sheep that is to slaughter led,
  Or lamb to shearer, so to them
  Not once His mouth He openëd
  At His trial in Jerusalem.'

THE PEARL

68

"In Jerusalem my Love was slain,
With shameless thieves on cross was rent;
Willing to suffer all men's pain,
The Man with all our griefs acquent;
His face so fair, from buffets ta'en,
Was there all torn and blood-besprent;
Sinless, yet He for sin could deign
To make Himself as naught; He lent
    His body to be scourged, and bent,
    And stretched, for us, on cruel beam;
    For us, meek lamb that made no plaint,
    He suffered in Jerusalem.

THE PEARL

Jerusalem, Jordan, and Galilee—
There baptized the good Saint John;
When Jesus coming he did see,
His words bore out Isaiah's own.
He said of Him this prophecy:
Behold God's Lamb, as true as stone,
Which taketh the iniquity
That all this world hath worked upon!'
   Though wrongs Himself had never done,
   All ours He claimed, was bruised for them.
   Who makes His generation known
   That died for us in Jerusalem?

70

"In Jerusalem, thus, to repeat
The witness true both Prophets bear,
Twice hailed as Lamb was my Lover sweet
So mild was His demeanour there.
And still the third time, as is meet,
Is in The Revelation, where,
Amidst the Throne, near Saints' high seat,
The Apostle saw Him clear and fair,
    Opening the book with leaves cut square
    And seven seals to seal the same;
    That sight made every creature fear,
    In Hell, in earth, and Jerusalem.

THE PEARL

XV

71

IN Jerusalem, eternally,
  All stainless white the Lamb Alive;
Such guarding of His purity
His wool's abundance doth contrive.
Hence, all souls of uncleanness free
Worthily with that Lamb shall wive.
Though many every day fetch He,
Yet never we together strive,—
    Save but, we would that each were five;
    The more the merrier, God me bless!
    Our love in numbers great can thrive,
    In honour more, and never less.

THE PEARL

"Less of bliss none can us bring
Who on our breast this pearl display;
Nor could those know an evil thing
Whom crowns of spotless pearls array.
Though there our corse lie mouldering,
And ye for grief cry without stay,
We know this: by one offering
Our hope is perfected for aye.
    The Lamb for us charms care away,
    At every feast makes mirthfulness;
    Most blest is each, most rich, most gay,
    And no one's honour ever less.

THE PEARL

73

"Less cogent that this may not sound,
Apocalypse shall teach you men.
'I saw,' says John, 'standing on ground
Of Sion's hill, the Lamb serene,
A hundred thousand maidens round,
And thousands four and four times ten.
On all their foreheads names I found
Of Lamb and Father. I heard then—
    Like voice of many waters when
    They rush in force, or on dark ness
    And tor the thunder leaps again—
    A mighty shout, than those not less.

74

" 'Nathless, above the tumult sharp,
Though louder had the voices grown,
A new song soon I heard them carp;
A purer, sweeter ne'er was known.
As harpers harping on the harp,
They sang that lay in clearest tone,
Nor did one tuneful measure warp,
Till echoes followed echoes flown.
    Right before God's very Throne,
    And those four Beasts which Him confess,
    And grave-faced Elders,—yet their own
    New song they sang there none the less.

THE PEARL

" 'Nathless, no men who sang or wrote,
For all the arts the wisest knew,
Of that one song could sing a note,
Except the Lamb's own retinue.
These, the redeemed, from earth remote,
As firstfruits unto God are due;
To the gentle Lamb they are devote,
As like Himself in look and hue.
    For never lie or tale untrue
    Once touched their lips in their distress.'
    Always their Master, stainless too,
    Unstained they now attend—no less."

THE PEARL

"Nathless," said I, "bear with me e'en
A little. If I a question pose,
'Tis not to try thy wit so keen,
Whom Christ to His own chamber chose.
My Pearl! —I am but clay unclean;
And thou so rich and brave a rose
Blowing where this fair bank is green
And joy of life no fainter grows.
   Gentle, who erstwhile didst enclose
   All simple graces, I would press
   One query. Rude am I, God knows,
   But grant my prayer, nevertheless,—

THE PEARL

XVI

77

NO less for this, my piteous prayer,
   If in thy choice it lie withal,
That thou art glorious, flawless-fair!
Have ye no homes in castle-wall,
No manor whither ye repair?
(Of Jerusalem thou tell'st; the hall
Of great King David's throne is there.
But in these groves—can it befall?—
   Lies city so imperial?
   Why, no, 'tis in Judaea old.)
   Like to yourselves, unblemished all,
   Should be the dwellings that you hold.

78

"To hold that spotless band, say I,
Those tens of thousands bright of face,
Some city large must be near-by,
For such a thronging populace.
That jewels gay unhoused should lie,
Untended, were too sad a case!
Yet buildings none can I espy,
As by this glorious brook I pace.
 Along its banks, a little space,
 For sweet seclusion ye have strolled.
 Elsewhere thy moated dwelling-place;
 Pray tell me of that fair stronghold."

THE PEARL

"The stronghold is in Judah's land,"
Said she, "of which but now ye spake,
The place He sought, ye understand,
To suffer in for mankind's sake—
Jerusalem the Old, for band
Of the old sin's thraldom there He brake.
The New, which God Himself then planned,
The Apostle John his theme did make.
 The Lamb, of black Who hath no flake,
 Led thither His flock—no need of fold!
 His nature all things there partake,
 And moatless is His safe freehold.

THE PEARL

80

"Two freeholds called Jerusalem
There are, to speak with carefulness;
And this the meaning of the name:
City of God or *Sight of Peace,*—
So called since Lamb of Bethlehem
Bled in the one for our release;
And who the other gain, for them
Is naught to glean but lasting peace.
  That is the town whereto we press,
  Our flesh once laid to rot in mould.
  There bliss and glory still increase
  To all the pure of His household."

81

"Gentle, withhold not this," reply
I made unto that lovely flower,
"But bring me where those buildings lie,
And let me see thy blissful bower."
"That prayer," she said, "God will deny;
Thou mayst not enter in His tower;
But the Lamb grants me a boon, whereby
Thou shalt have outward sight, this hour,
    Of that clear cloister's walls—no more;
    No foot of ground that they enfold.
    To walk those streets thou hast no power,
    Unclean, beyond that clean threshold.

THE PEARL

XVII

82

"TO see that stronghold, now thou mayst
   Thy footsteps turn toward this brook's
(As I on this bank, thee abreast),
Till to a hill thou find'st thee led."
I waited not, but slipping past
The leafy branches, on I sped,
And from a height I saw at last,
Still pressing forward, that Homestead.
   Beyond the brook, before me spread,
   With rays more bright than sun's it shone,
   As in Apocalypse he said
   He saw it once, the Apostle John.

THE PEARL

83

As John the Apostle with own eyes' sight,
I saw that City great in fame,
From Heaven royally bedight
Come down, the New Jerusalem.
The City was of pure gold, bright
Like burnished glass, it shone as flame;
Set firm on precious stones aright,
Twelve rows of these; and rich of frame
 Foundation-courses, twelve the same,
 Each separate tier a different stone—
 Magnificent, as doth proclaim
 In Apocalypse the Apostle John.

THE PEARL

84

From John's words of the Citadel,
I knew how named those stones had been:
Jasper, the first, discerned I well,
It gleamed in lowest course so green;
Above it how they rose, to tell,—
Sapphire held the next gradine;
Third, chalcedon, that none excel
In purity, so pale and clean;
    Emerald green, the fourth therein;
    And sardonyx its neighbour stone;
    The ruby sixth, as he had seen
    In Apocalypse, the Apostle John.

THE PEARL

To them John adds the chrysolite,
The seventh circumambient;
The eighth, the beryl clear and white;
The topaz, ninth, twin colours pent;
The chrysoprase the tenth is hight;
Eleventh, jacinth excellent;
The twelfth, of all the fairest quite,
Amethyst, blue and purple blent.
    The wall above, a sheer ascent
    Of jasper, crystal-clear that shone,
    As taught me had New Testament,
    The Apocalypse of Apostle John.

THE PEARL

What John described, still saw I there.
The twelve great steps were broad and steep;
Above them stood the City, square
Each way—as long as broad as deep;
Gold streets that shone like glass lay bare,
From jasper wall the light did leap;
Within, adorned the dwellings were
With precious stones, each kind an heap.
    That fastness every way did keep
    A full twelve thousand furlongs on;
    Of height, of breadth, of length the sweep
    He saw them measured, Apostle John!

THE PEARL

XVIII

87

YET more I saw, as John told well:
  The City's walls had each three gates
(Twelve to those precincts I could tell),
Adorned with richly fashioned plates;
Each portal, indefectible,
A pearl whose lustre ne'er abates;
With names of sons of Israel
Inscribed, in order due of dates,
  As after him had been their fates
  By birth to follow long or soon.
  Such light there shone in all the streets,
  Those dwellers needed sun nor moon.

THE PEARL

88

For sun nor moon no need to cry:
Their lamplight God Himself, unspent;
The Lamb their lantern sure, whereby
The City gleaméd, translucent.
No bar was wall or house to eye,
Such clarity the aether lent;
And there one saw the Throne Most High,
Arrayed with all the apparelment
   That John by words did represent;
    The High God's Self sat on the Throne.
   From out of it a river went,
    More bright than both the sun and moon.

THE PEARL

89

Shone never sun or moon so sweet
As from that floor the plenteous flood;
Swiftly it swept through every street,
But left no trace of slime or mud.
No church had there been built, nor yet
Chapel or temple or altar-rood;
The Almighty was their Minster meet,
The Lamb their Sacrifice and Food.
    Not barred at street the great gates stood,
    But open still, high noon to noon;
    And enter there no creature could
    Who bears a spot beneath the moon.

THE PEARL

90

To the moon from it accrues no might;
A thing too spotted, she, and grim;
And there, besides, is never night:
Why should the moon her circle climb
And seek to match the glorious light
That breaks upon that brook's far brim?
The planets are in too poor a plight,
And the sun himself is much too dim. . . .
  Bright trees that grow along the stream
  Twelve fruits of life bear, late and soon,
  Twelve times a year, with laden limb,
  And are renewed at every moon.

THE PEARL

91

Beneath the moon is heart too frail
For man of flesh to live and see,
As I in trance, that gleaming Pale
Ineffable in mystery.
I stood, dazed as a couching quail,
Its strangeness so transported me,
Till sense of rest or toil did fail,
Or aught but purest ecstasy.
    For I dare say, if bodily
    A mortal man had known that boon,
    Let him in cure of all clerks be,
    His life were lost beneath the moon.

THE PEARL

XIX

92

AS when the mighty moon doth rise
Before day's light is all gone down,
I was aware in sudden wise
Of a procession. Summons none
Had been, but straightway companies
Flowed through that City of renown—
Of virgin hosts in self-same guise
As was my Pearl with orient crown.
  The like had each of them, and gown,
  With pearls adorned, of purest white;
  And each displayed, her breast upon,
  The pearl of bliss and great delight.

THE PEARL

With movements light I saw them tread
The golden streets that shone as glass,
Those hundred-thousands habited
In liveries of one rank and class;
And all were joyful. At their head
Proudly the Lamb of God did pass,
His seven horns of gold clear red;
As though of pearls His mantle was.
    To the Throne come near, they did not press,
    But held their ordered way aright;
    As mild as modest maids at Mass,
    That host moved on with great delight.

THE PEARL

94

The deep delight His coming made
Were theme too great for mortal tongue.
Their foreheads low the Elders laid
As He drew nearer with His throng.
Legions of angels, summonëd,
Sweet odours from their censers flung.
Then the Jewel's praise afresh was paid
In glorious glee from voices strong.
    Strike through earth to Hell, that song
    Of the heavenly Virtues' chorus might.
    And I, my voice His host's among,
    I praised the Lamb with deep delight.

THE PEARL

Delight, with wonder, filled my mind:
What words to tell His praises in?
Most gentle He, most blithe, most kind,
Of whom I e'er heard speech begin.
His raiment white, His looks inclined
Toward all with love, all souls would win;
But oh! His heart with gash was lined,
Where broad wet wound had rent the skin;
    From white side came the blood within.
    Alas! thought I, who did that spite?
    For burnt with grief breast should have been
    That in such outrage took delight.

THE PEARL

96

The Lamb's delight could plain be seen.
Not face or bearing once bewrayed
How sorely wounded He had been;
Gladness in all His glances played.
I scanned His troop; and every mien
Life's utter fulness quickenéd.
Then saw I there my little queen,
Whom I thought near me in the glade.
    And Lord! what mirth was that she made
    Among her fellows, she so white!
    It gave me thought across to wade
    For deep love-longing and delight.

THE PEARL

XX

97

DELIGHT me drove, of eye and ear;
My human mind with madness ailed.
I longed to be there with my dear,
Beyond the brook from me withheld.
At naught that might a man deter,
Nor blow nor wrench, my courage quailed;
With my purpose none should interfere—
To plunge and swim, though death assailed!
Roughly that venture was curtailed.
When I, possessed beyond all measure,
Made as to start, back I was haled.
'Twas not to be my Prince's pleasure.

THE PEARL

98

'Twas not His pleasure I should dash
Through river many-marvellëd
In frantic haste. So hot and rash,
How quickly was I quieted!
One leap toward where those waters wash—
It snatched me from my dream instead. . . .
In garden-plot, awake, in the flesh,
On that same mound still lay my head
    Whereon my pearl to earth had strayed.
    I stretched; and then I felt a seizure
    Of fright upon me, sighed, and said,
    "Now all be to that Prince's pleasure."

THE PEARL

But pleasured ill to be so soon
Outcast from all those regions fair
Of glowing life, I fell in swoon,
For longing to revisit there;
And cried, as to that blessëd one,
"O Pearl of rich renown so rare,
Precious to me thy words, and boon
Of this true dream. If so it were
    That thou in garland gay roam'st where
    I saw thee in thy joyful leisure,
    O well to me, grief's prisoner,
    That thou art of the Prince's pleasure!"

THE PEARL

To the Prince's pleasure had I bent,
Nor sought what He did not bestow,
And held me in that firm intent,
As the Pearl had prayed me,—then, I trow,
Belike unto God's presence sent,
More mysteries I had witnessed so.
But always man is exigent
Of much that right did ne'er him owe.
    Thus soon joy left me, here below,
    Outcast from timeless realms of azure.
    Lord, mad are they who against Thee go,
    Or proffer aught against Thy pleasure.

THE PEARL

His peace, His pleasure—end and ground
Of each true Christian man's design—
They are not hard. In Him I found
A God, a Lord, a Friend benign. . . .
Such was my lot where, on that mound,
I mourned the pearl that had been mine,
And yielded it to God, and bound
It fast in Christ's dear name and sign,
    Who comes to us in bread and wine
    Each day.—Grant us His gifts to treasure,
    As servants of His House divine,
    And precious pearls unto His pleasure.
                    Amen. Amen.

BIBLIOGRAPHY

BIBLIOGRAPHY

Bibliography

(The following list is a selected one. Fuller references to books and articles on *The Pearl* will be found in several of the works cited below.)

I. FACSIMILE EDITION OF THE MANUSCRIPT OF THE FOUR POEMS

Pearl, Cleanness, Patience and Sir Gawain, reproduced in facsimile from the unique MS. Cotton Nero A. x in the British Museum, with introduction by Sir I. Gollancz . . . Early English Text Society. Oxford, 1923.

II. MODERN EDITIONS

A. Of *The Pearl*:

The Pearl, a Middle English Poem, edited with introduction, notes, and glossary, by Charles G. Osgood, Jr., Ph.D. Boston and London, 1906.

Pearl, an English Poem of the XIVth Century: edited with modern rendering, together with Boccaccio's *Olympia,* by Sir Israel Gollancz. London, 1921.

The Pearl (*The Bowdoin Edition*), *The Text of the Fourteenth Century English Poem,* edited by members of the Chaucer course . . . in Bowdoin College. Boston, 1932.

B. Of the other poems in the manuscript:

Purity, a Middle English Poem, edited with introduction, notes, and glossary, by Robert J. Menner. New Haven, 1920.

Patience, a West Midland Poem of the Fourteenth Century, edited with introduction, bibliography, notes, and glossary, by Hartley Bate-

[107]

son. Manchester, 1912. [Second edition, recast and partly rewritten, 1918.]

Sir Gawain and the Green Knight, edited by J. R. R. Tolkien and E. V. Gordon. Oxford, 1925. [Corrected impression, 1930.]

III. MODERN RENDERINGS

The Pearl: an Anonymous English Poem of the 14th Century rendered in prose, by Charles G. Osgood, Jr., Ph.D. [Privately printed.] Princeton, 1907.

The Pearl, a Middle English Poem: a modern version in the metre of the original, by Sophie Jewett. New York, 1908.

Romance, Vision and Satire, edited by Jessie L. Weston. Boston and New York, 1912. [Contains verse renderings of *The Pearl* and *Gawain* entire and of portions of *Cleanness* and *Patience*.]

Sir Gawain and the Green Knight, translated by Theodore Howard Banks, Jr. New York, 1929.

IV. LINGUISTIC AND METRICAL STUDIES

C. S. Northup, "Study of the Metrical Structure of *The Pearl*," *Pub. Mod. Lang. Assn.*, XII (1897), 326-340.

K. Schumacher, *Studien über den Stabreim in der Mittelenglischen Alliterationsdichtung*. Bonn, 1914.

Margaret P. Medary, "Stanza-Linking in Middle English Verse," *Romanic Review*, VII (1916), 243-270.

O. F. Emerson, "Imperfect Lines in *Pearl*," etc., *Modern Philology*, XIX (1921), 131-139.

BIBLIOGRAPHY

O. F. Emerson, "Some Notes on the Pearl," *PMLA*, XXXVII (1922), 52-93.

——— "More Notes on *Pearl*," *Ibid.*, XLII (1927), 807-831.

V. BIOGRAPHICAL AND CRITICAL STUDIES

Introductions to editions by Osgood and Gollancz, listed above.

Carleton Brown, "The Author of *The Pearl*, considered in the Light of his Theological Opinions," *PMLA*, XIX (1904), 115-153.

W. H. Schofield, (I) "The Nature and Fabric of *The Pearl*," *Ibid.*, XIX (1904), 154-215.

G. G. Coulton, "In Defense of 'Pearl,'" *Modern Language Review*, II (1906), 39-43.

I. Gollancz, in *Cambridge History of English Literature*, 1907, Vol. I, Ch. XV. [Bibliography, 525-526.]

Katharine Lee Bates, in *The Dial* (Chicago), XLV (1908), 450-452. [Review of translations by Miss Jewett and Miss Mead.]

W. H. Schofield, (II) "Symbolism, Allegory, and Autobiography in *The Pearl*," *PMLA*, XXIV (1909), 585-675.

Robert M. Garrett, "*The Pearl*: an Interpretation," *University of Washington Publications in English*, Vol. IV, No. 1. Seattle, 1918.

J. B. Fletcher, "The Allegory of *The Pearl*," *Journal of English and Germanic Philology*, XX (1921), 1-22.

Edmund Gosse, *More Books on the Table* (London, 1923), 179-186.

Sister M. Madeleva, *Pearl: a Study in Spiritual Dryness*. New York and London, 1925.

THE PEARL

W. K. Greene, *"The Pearl*—a New Interpretation," *PMLA*, XL (1925), 814-827.

Elizabeth Hart, "The Heaven of Virgins," *Modern Language Notes*, XLII (1927), 113-116.

Oscar Cargill and Margaret Schlauch, *"The Pearl* and its Jeweler," *PMLA*, XLIII (1928), 105-122.

C. O. Chapman, (I) "The Musical Training of the Pearl Poet," *PMLA*, XLVI (1931), 177-181.

—— (II) "The Authorship of *The Pearl*," *Ibid.*, XLVII (1932), 346-353.

Of this edition of THE PEARL *one thousand copies have been printed on natural wove paper and fifty copies on handmade paper by Fred Anthoensen, The Southworth Press, Portland, Maine.*

139